Standing
around
the Heart

Standing around the Heart

Poems by
Gary Fincke

The University of Arkansas Press
Fayetteville
2005

09   08   07   06   05   5   4   3   2   1

Designed by Ellen Beeler

☉ The paper used in this publication meets the minimum
requirements of the American National Standard for
Permanence of Paper for Printed Library Materials
Z39.48-1984.

Library of Congress Cataloging-in-Publication Data

Fincke, Gary.
  Standing around the heart : poems / by Gary Fincke.
    p. cm.
  ISBN 1-55728-786-4 (pbk. : alk. paper)
  I. Title.
  PS3556.I457S73 2005
  811'.54—dc22

                                        2004017985

For Derek, Shannon, Aaron, Gavin, Raea,
and especially for Liz

Acknowledgments

"The History of SAC," *Boulevard*; "Sweet Things," *DoubleTake*; "Bringing Back the Bones," *The Georgia Review;* "Liverwurst, Headcheese, a List of Loaves," "The Signs of Life on Mars," *The Gettysburg Review*; "Descending with Bagpipes," *Green Mountains Review*; "The Half-Dream of the Dolphin," *The Iowa Review*; "The Doors of Hell," "The Top Bunk of a Ford," *The Literary Review*; "Becoming Someone," *The Louisville Review*; "Zombies," *Mankato Poetry Review;* "The Uses of Rain," "Coughing through the Brambles," "During Sixth Grade," *The Missouri Review*; "Standing around the Heart," "The Eternal Language of the Hands," Johnny Weissmuller Learns the Tarzan Yell," "Miss Hartung Teaches the Importance of Fruit," "Dialogues," *The Paris Review*; "The Elephant Paintings," *Poetry*; "In the House without Fables," "In Films, the Army Ants are Always Intelligent," *Poetry Northwest;* "Finding Harvey Kelly in the Former Sanitarium," *Press;* "The Buchinger Limbs," "Leaving," "Moving the Rain" "Bird Elegy," "The Museum of Memory," "The Weaknesses of the Mouth," "Anniversary" "Giants," "The Details of the Soil," *The Southern Review*; "The History of Silk," *Western Humanities Review.*

Contents

*Standing
around
the
Heart*

Standing around the Heart

We stood, in health class, around the cow's heart
Miss Hutchings unwrapped on her desk. Inside
And out, she said, we need to know ourselves,
Halving that heart to show us auricles,
Ventricles, valves, the walls well built or else.
Her fingers found where arteries begin.
She pressed the ends of veins. Richard Turner,
Whose father's heart had halted, examined
His hands. Anne Cole, whose father had revived
To cut hair at the mall, stepped back, turning
From the outlet to the steer's aorta,
The four chambers we were required to know.
While we watched, Miss Hutchings unwrapped the hearts
Of chickens and turkeys, the hearts of swine
And sheep, arranged them by size on the thick,
Brown sack, leaving a space, we knew, for ours.
We took our pulses. We listened by way
Of her stethoscopes, to each other, boy
To boy, girl to girl, because of the chance
We'd touch. Those butcher hearts warmed while I dreamed
Of pressing my ear to the rhythmic heart
Of Stephanie Romig, whose breasts, so far,
Had brushed me one time while dancing. And then
Miss Hutchings recited the quart total
Of our blood, the distance it must travel,

Leaving and returning, all of the names
For the necessary routes it followed,
Ending with capillaries so close
To the surface we could nearly reach them
With our lips and tongues, rushing blood to each
Of the sweet, sensitive sources for joy.

The Eternal Language of the Hands

The surgeon Celsus, at the time of Christ,
Said the right hand should operate
On the left eye, the left hand should invade
The right. He meant the interns to practice
From the weak side like switch-hitters,
An old strategy which makes us smile.
But the smug health of the moment
Turns a page in the book of longing:
I looked left, then right, at the pictures
My father showed me—the husband, the wife,
Through five generations which ended
In German scrawled unintelligibly
Across the back. I was young enough
To believe, because he had lived
With grandparents who spoke privately
In German, he would translate the three pairs
Born somewhere other than Pittsburgh.
I expected a second language to
Enter me like the left-handed layup
I practiced each day, but he said German
Was forbidden like taking the Lord's name
In vain, that he'd shaken off Kraut and Hun
And Heine, slurs I'd never hear because
His parents had changed themselves. Consider
How many cataracts Celsus removed,

Inserting his needles, nudging them
Off-center like wind-blown grit. Left, then
Right-handed, thousands of years before
The surgeries we wait for. My father
The baker rolled sandwich buns with both hands
At once, circles so tight you couldn't tell
Which had been formed from the left or right,
Like Celsus removing clouds and teaching
Those miracles to disciples
In the eternal language of the hands.

The Buchinger Limbs

In the year I wrote small, everything
I knew could be copied on a page
If I practiced until I mastered
The perfect penmanship to succeed.
A corner for school, thin lines along
The bottom where lust and pleasure spoke.
Inch of family, a column of friends,
The short sentences of school and work.
I was a tenth-grade wonder, shrinking
Myself to stumps of ink, until my aunt
Told me tales of Matthew Buchinger,
The man with flippers for arms and legs
Who wrote seven Psalms and The Lord's Prayer
As the curls of his self-portrait hair,
Reducing those articles of faith
To miracles of calligraphy.
So tiny, she said, each of those words.
Think of holding the pen with a fin,
Using that grip for the common sense
Of achievement. On the news, reports
Of thalidomide. In Germany,
Where her father had come from, cases
Of the newborn with Buchinger limbs.
Look, she told me, so many deformed
We will soon not notice the dreadful.
If you can learn anything at all,
The smallest words will drive you blind.

Falling down Stairs

Sunday afternoon, I'm four-years-old
And clumsy in new corrective shoes.
What I am watching from the back porch
Is an old man, a stranger, leaning
On a polished black cane in the yard.
When I finish tumbling down the stairs,
He is tilted over me, getting
No closer than cane's length, and moaning
In the slurred, foreign language of stroke.
Listening and listening, I feel
I've woken up changed into a dog
That waits to hear the one word it knows.
My father, kneeling, turns me into
A boy who can not cry; my mother
Ties my shoe before he carries me.
I ride my father's arms up thirteen
Wooden stairs to the door that opens
To an uncle and cousins who stare
Like a congregation. They watch me
As if my body has turned the green
Of the shoe store's fluoroscope, and they
Can see how the necessary parts
Of me are still intact and fitted.
And when I answer the first question
With my name, there is such a shuffling

Of voices I know I've returned from
Closely watched sleep, a child become mouth
And nose and eyes, practically a moon,
So still that anyone wishing for
Its face to change believes it is stone.

The Uses of Rain

We sat, in geography, for nine weeks
With water, a marking period of rain.
We followed the dittoed diagrams
Of water's efficient recycling:
Precipitation, evaporation,
All the clouds we memorized for exams—
Cirrus, cumulus, the great thunderheads
Like the ones Mr. Sanderson called us
To watch at the windows. Snow, he told us,
Was nature's cheap ice cream, more air in drifts
Than water. A barometer, he said,
Could thrive inside an injured knee. And he
Made us read the names for irrigation,
How crop rotation and the geometry
Of plowing could safety-net the earth.
He taught the proper times for lawn sprinklers,
The folly of building in the flood plain,
And we remembered the timetables
For tides, the value of delta, wetlands,
And the extraordinary ecosystem
Of the ocean. And though we conserved
For extra credit, though we cataloged
Our care, we took our test, turned it in,
And listened, books closed, to Mr. Sanderson
Tell us the story of the crested bustard,

Whose desire is triggered by the sound of rain.
"Because it lives in the desert," he explained,
"Its courtship dance must be timed just right."
He held our stack of tests to his chest
And walked among our rows. "In zoos," he said,
"In captivity, those birds begin to dance
When they hear a keeper's hose. They prance
To the simple sound of cleaning, believing
That rain will water the luck of their children."

Sweet Things

All the way through doughnuts I sang along
With the radio because they were the last
Sweet things I laid my hands on before my shift
Was over. My father was busy with icing,
Blending color with different degrees of sugar,
And then he had an hour of pastries to fill
With custard and fruit to compete with the rolls
On television which cakewalked to the oven.
In the bakery, time raised bread and browned it.
Time hand-rolled sandwich buns, carried pies
And coffee cakes to cool on countertops,
None of them strutting off their pans after
I stepped into snow, inhaling with the joy
I thought I'd earned before dawn, driving
The station wagon four miles to where
My mother was drinking sugared coffee
And eating zwieback she'd brought home stale
The night before. I heard news, weather,
And the drive-time deejay say Bobby Vee,
Connie Francis, or some sound-alike
For success because it was time for
The world to go to reasonable work.
And I left that car on the plowed street
So I could say the hell with shoveling
Our driveway with the snow still falling,

Exhaling with my mother before she closed
The door on the Chevy still warm and steered
It back to the bakery in the changing light
To sell to men finishing one shift
Or starting another at the mill,
Each carrying a bag of sweet things
Into the ordinary ends of morning.

Bringing Back the Bones

I read about the men who maim themselves,
Who amputate fingers and toes and arms:
The man who practiced on pork shoulders and
Put, finally, the shotgun to his leg;
The man who crushed his leg, set it afire;
The multiple cases of men who laid
Their legs across railroad tracks and waited
As if the world has insufficient loss.
I remember two friends who lost both legs
In cars, others who gave up toes and feet
To diabetes. I want to write them
Whole, bringing back the bones, though my father,
Each time I visit, reminds me my words
Are no different than bread he baked, the cakes
He iced by hand, squeezing out the sweet script
Of birthday names. He shows me, this trip,
The school bus full of old books and papers,
Tells me he's driving them to Aspinwall
For dollars by the ton. We stand, later,
In the leveled lot of the razed bakery.
He scuffs one mark for the workbench, one more
For the mixer, nods at my shoes and waits
Where the dough would rise, while I toe the earth
And tell him my tale of the wooden legs
On the child mummy unwrapped in Egypt,

The carbon-dating which said those legs were
Centuries younger than her bones, someone
Opening the grave and fitting those legs,
Someone forming sized feet from reeds and mud.

In the House without Fables

In the house without fables
the animals were unhappy.
The dog did nothing but bark.
The cats muttered literal mews.

On their orange plastic wheels,
the hamsters spun and spun
until the terrible times brought
stories not ending with lessons.

Smoke floated nowhere but downwind.
Twilight was always the start
of darkness and the night noises
of sex and hunger, all the wings

flapping in the awful flight
of the domestic turkey.
From the second-story windows
of that house, from our bedrooms,

we watched the nearest neighbors.
Across the darknesses
between us and their rooms,
we imagined the weak lights

of myth. They might have been
televisions flickering through
the evenings, or else we saw
nothing when the youngest died

but the raccoon which clawed
at our curled drainpipe, stuck
just outside our window,
its teeth bared at our sudden light.

The Half-Dream of the Dolphin

The brain of the dolphin shuts down one
hemisnhere at a time.

My sister tells me the portrait is free,
That she wants, for once, a professional lens
To seal us together; and, in this dream
The blessing of excuses is so muted
I go without debating, early off
The elevator with luminous families
Who clutch coupons, file to floodlights and patter
While I stand and sit, stand and sit, stand and see
Our mother, years dead, climbing the stairs, silent,
Refusing support, and I want to shout,
"Slowly!" or "Go back!" or curse my sister,
The nurse, who believes the dreamed have no disease,
Doesn't see the picture that must be taken
Is this shot of our mother on the stairs
Repeating soft *no*s to her heart, ignoring
The curfew of her image until she sits
Slack-mouthed and sideways on the mall's last landing.
Instead of speaking, my sister blinks out.
Instead of acting, I wake to the sleepless
Half of dying, to believing someone
Has sense in the sequel, the lost episode
With the studio downstairs, the descent
Through the sea-chapter of sleep to that depth
Where, just before memory goes dark, it stays
Another moment, convincingly bright.

Leaving

So many stories I've read, lately,
About a father or mother or both
Leaving a child behind. At rest stops.
At gas stations or malls or simply,
This week, on a city street, the mother
Saying "Wait here, don't move" and entering
The store which sells alternate futures.
My father, once, in anger, stopped
The car he was driving and opened
His door, not mine, getting out and walking
The opposite way. I followed him
In the mirror because I would not turn,
And he faced away from me and that car
I'd driven just twice. He must have been
Deciding what he'd do if I didn't
Pull away, how long he could walk before
Turning around was impossible,
But I slid over, finally, and
Shifted into first, letting the clutch out
Smoother than I ever had, feeding
The gas, and ten minutes later, telling
My mother nothing except he'd gone
For a walk, leaving things up to him.
But eleven years later, while my son
Stared at toys, I stepped behind a pillar,

And when he looked back where I was supposed
To be, I watched him turn circles as if
He'd erase himself with fear. The aisles were
Unsolvable, the doors unreachable
As moons. There was no voice for excuse,
And each ridiculous reason
I had for anything turned mute.

The Signs of Life on Mars

When Mrs. Sowers showed us the Canals of Mars,
She traced the straight lines of them with the rubber tip
Of a wooden pointer and repeated Erie,
Panama, and Suez, starting a list we should
Memorize for one week's worth of geography.
Likely, she said, there were countries on Mars which fought
Over their technological marvels, and she
Named the nations threatening war for the Suez,
Explained the domino effect to the A-bomb,
And died years before someone saw, in photographs
From a space probe, the mile-wide Great Stone Face of Mars,
Eye and nose and mouth in profile like a thousand
Expressioned stones on Earth. So like us, the faithful
Murmured, reading the rock for racial clues, seeing,
In another photo, a Martian Happy Face,
Its huge smile stretching five miles like a miracle
Of kitsch, the aliens signaling A-OK
As if they'd evolved, just like us, from the microbes
Believed, this year, to be fossilized in ancient
Martian boulders. Here are the miniscule feces
Of bacteria; here, carbonates, magnetite.
My wife gives her fourth graders a short article,
Adjusted for age, which summarizes the signs
Of life on Mars, no mention of Percival Lowell,
The atlas he drew of Martian infrastructure,

How once, in February, when Mrs. Sowers
Had her husband, an engineer, show us a film
On the first turnpike in America because
Part of it ran through our township, he told our class
Those lines weren't canals at all, just Martian forests
Which flourished on either side, how irrigation
Would show itself to approaching spacecraft, how growth
Along turnpikes would tell the monsters we could think.

The Unthinkable

The unthinkable, my father said,
Was the steel mill closing, a mile
Of buildings given up to vandals
While the rest of us packed to leave.

He sold bread and pastries to families
Who could sell their homes to no one,
Repeating himself because my teachers
Were training me for the A-bomb,

Touting the worth of duck and cover,
Encouraging bottled water,
Canned goods, a stockpile of batteries
For a radio underground.

Think of the unthinkable, they said,
And I did, expecting Pittsburgh,
Seven miles away, to vanish while
I cowered to cover my eyes.

One of those scenarios came true.
It took months for every window
In the closed mill to be broken, years
Before the bakery foundered.

The unthinkable moved to Cuba;
My father moved to maintenance
At the high school where I waited for
Buttons on a blouse to open

And worried that Soviet missiles
Would arc into Pennsylvania
Before I could enter any girl.
I thought I deserved some pleasure

For being born the same morning
As the A-bomb, unhooking a bra
So slowly my breathing seemed pillowed
By desire. And just then, that girl

Told me *of course* there was a future,
That she was saving herself as part
Of God's Catholic plan, her faith sounding
So childish I could only cover

Her mouth and enter her warm, damp hand
Because, in there, nothing sacred
Could be torn while I kept disbelief,
So unthinkable, to myself.

Anniversary

We learn, today, a girl who attended
Our wedding has been murdered. Thirty years,
We say, guessing her age—eleven? twelve?—
From the old photographs that help us tell.

We read the articles from three papers—
Cord-strangled, the saw taken to her limbs—
One picture, then another, something like
A legend beginning, something like hell.

Just home with her fiancé, our daughter
Looks at our young selves. The summer evening
Reaches into our kitchen; she helps us
Name the naturally dead, chanting a spell

For her mother's white gown, what my daughter
Will wear, this gift she tries on, beginning
To enter her story, raising the sleeves
To her face, drawing them closer to smell.

Moving the Rain

When I read about the priest who refused
To baptize a boy named Damien, citing
The child born to become the Antichrist
In the three *Omen* movies, I remembered
My father telling me the wild pansy
Is *heartsease,* that I should know the old names
Of the natural world, how they are arranged.
He was giving in to surgery after
Years of self-treatment; a friend, that summer,
Locked his garage and idled inside until
He darkened his choice on the machine-scored test
Of *How and When.* Although who could say what
Impossibly he wanted, his garage
Arranged alphabetically as if he were
Selling his home to the librarian
Of cars and gardens. How literally
We take ourselves, my daughter showing me
The woman who sweeps her sidewalk three times
Per day, who draws her broom across her driveway
To rid it of the grit of several hours.
And when it rains, she spreads the puddles,
Returning at nine and one and six, sweeping
In the dark of December, moving the rain.

False Reads

*False alerts of Soviet missiles in flight occurred
on November 9, 1979, June 3 and 6, 1980*

Like rice thrown from a hand, those blips
Say missiles are married to their targets.
In front of those screens, soldiers move
From one to another to whispering
With men who evaluate the long odds
Such lights are errors. They fumble
Loose the keys that unlock the end of things.

When soldiers dream this moment,
They wish for the false read and wake
To a confusion of brilliance. They send
Their futures off with suitcases, repeat
The "don't look back" of longing.
They begin the countdown to launch,
Deciding all the weather of the world.

Time catches in their throats, sticking
Like inhaled meat. Those men revert
To the ancient gestures of eyes and hands,
The reflexive signs for need. And then,
Suddenly, all those screens turn unblemished
As perfect CAT scans, missiles, perhaps, spit
And polished away by collective prayer.

Later, some of those soldiers admit
To sudden doubt. That they believed those blips
Were real despite the graphs gone blank.
That they thought the Soviets had launched a fog
Of emptiness across their screens to hide
The signals that were screaming just above
The thin, false ceiling of security.

That they waited and watched the clear beauty
That spread from the dark fissure of politics,
Following the sweep hands buckled to their wrists
As if taking the weak pulse of hopelessness.

Becoming Someone

Irezumi—the Japanese art of full-body tattoos

In Tokyo, you visit
The tattoo museums to read
The texts by needles and ink.
Hundreds of human skins hang
Like art, and you're embarrassed
By your small, discreet design.
Irezumi, you murmur,
And though the fully tattooed
Live shorter lives, though inked skin
Must struggle to breathe, you call
The homes of listed artists.

Already you're becoming
Someone nobody can change.
After you're decorated,
You'll walk in that skin and be
Literal and permanent.
The world won't have to make up
Its mind about you. Not now.
Not when you have anted up
For an afterlife. You saw
Those crowds reading the old skins.
Everything they repeated
Sounded the same. The symbols

You have chosen mean something
So exact you will never
Be interpreted again.

The Elephant Paintings

Once a week, at the Phoenix Zoo,
Ruby, the elephant artist,
Fills another canvas. Keepers
Bring an easel, brushes, the jars
Of acrylic paint, and she waits,
As she must, while elephant aides
Flutter her studio ready.

Now she taps a jar with her trunk;
Now she chooses a certain brush,
And one of the handlers dips it
In paint, passes it to that snout
Which slathers color. Swing and stroke—
Some Sundays Ruby works one brush;
Some Sundays Ruby switches hues.
But when she steps back, ten minutes
Or less, she's finished, and nothing
Can convince Ruby to revise.

The accidental avant-garde,
We hazard, smiling at the price
On signed, limited editions
Of lithographs, nothing under
Two hundred and fifty dollars.
But her handlers, while we watch, pull

An unpicked brush, offer the wrong
Color, and Ruby refuses,
Her artistry explained, we're told,
By the luminosity of
Pigments theory, psychologists
And ophthalmologists pointing
Out the expressionistic joy
In varying, sealed shades of gray,
Enough faux-rainbow to dazzle
The critic who claims her lines are
Classic Japanese, delicate
On nearly empty canvas. Though
The ones the zoo displays are bright
And bold, all of them abstracts, what
We'd expect from an elephant
Who's painting in captivity,
Not in touch, ever, with her free,
Yet representational peers.

Bird Elegy

In post-apocalypse stories, when more
Than roaches survive, one woman remains
In the ruined world, and always she's found
By surviving men who cross continents,
Sail oceans, or stumble from a nearby,
Accidental shield of lead. The woman
Chooses strength and goodness; and thankfully,
She's young and healthy and gorgeous herself,
Able to give birth like the animals
Without worrying about Down syndrome
Or the consequences of suspect genes
When everything's up to her like it was
For the last female black robin on Earth.
For what hope was there, that bird already
Older than its ordinary life span?
What could she expect from the final males?
Yet she has two hundred descendants, more
To come, the sentimental name "Old Blue."
Although we know it's not love for the man
Or the species, it's the need in ourselves,
The old desire to be fondled and touched
Exactly there, and yes, there, for the joy
That makes us heroic, frees the noises
We leak, then gladly flood into the air.

The
Doors
of
Hell

The Doors of Hell

For more than forty years an underground mine
fire has burned beneath Centralia, Pennsylvania,
nearly all of which has been abandoned

Driving through Centralia

The hot spots are stars
that drift far from where
the earth once opened,
allowing a boy
to slide toward fire.
The roots which saved him
are a tourist site.
The families who
have moved are erased,
their houses become
streets of empty lots.

The Aeneas Tour

The priests of Avernus descended into Hell.
Trip after trip, black-clad and cowled, they guided
The paying by torchlight to the underground
River which ran from the volcano's hot springs.
They counted on the length and depth of a cave
Constructed for the Oracle of the Dead;
They relied on awe and drugs when they halted
Where the steam clouds roiled the tunnel hazy.

The pilgrims believed they'd reached the River Styx,
The priests chanting under the wavering lamps.
Later, after his tour, Virgil remembered
The stream's passage to fog, the hooded boatman,
Though he writes nothing about how many years
It took to build Hell's tunnel three hundred yards
Through rock, how perfectly the earliest priests
Predicted the dreaded water. And what of
The priests who astonished him, those who played
The spirits of the dead, becoming the friends
And relatives of pilgrims? What faith they had,
Repeating the tours, accepting the money
While Hades lay elsewhere. There was vocation,
Nothing in their downslope promoting hope, not
For the priest who rowed the boat, the monk who wailed
Laments until they reascended to sit
Across from each other through silent suppers.

The DOH Club

All winter my mother showed me Hell,
Opening the furnace, shoveling
The coal while my father slept toward
The making of pastries and pies.
"The devil's work," she said, tossing in
The daily trash, "and you'll roast in it
Unless you're good," and I believed her
Because every paper I covered
With crayoned pictures curled and went black.
Nothing of me lasted as long as bread.

The snow piled up one weekend until
Everyone walked again, heads tilted
Into the wind. On steep Gibson Hill
A boy on a sled surprised a truck
And was split like crust. I stayed inside
And dreamed my skin would tear, letting loose
My soul. My room above the furnace
Grew horns; my spirit was coal. And then,
In North Korea, somebody else
We knew was opened as easily
As a dinner roll. All afternoon
Our radio said his name, the tubes
In the back glowing like the letters
On my father's bakery sign.

It was seven blocks to where the mill
Made its hell renovations, the hills
Which flared, then faded, ready to be
Hauled to the waste pits. The Doors of Hell,
According to my aunt, were downstairs,
One block from that furnace. At dusk, men
I didn't know filled the DOH,
Men who thought they would leave by midnight
And stayed so long their wives replaced them,
Saying nothing about their secret sense
Of that nearby passage to hell, clearing
Their throats for the lost languages
Of Eastern Europe, spitting sooted phlegm,
Beginning the stories which ended
In the guttural names for fire.

Subsidence, Mine Fire, the Tomb of Eve

*For thirty years, a woman spoke from
the supposed tomb of Eve in Jeddah,
answering questions from religious
pilgrims.*

In the *Encyclopedia Britannica,*
For three editions, paragraphs
About the Salem Church Dam, height
And length, the power and purpose
Of the never-constructed, some
Fact-checker believing it built,
That a reservoir rose behind it.
Like hell ready for the day of moving.
Like the huge hole which opened
Outside my classroom window, stopped
Three feet short of the brickwork wall.
Coal mine, certainly. Underground fire.
But for all I knew, the sudden suck
Of collapse would widen past ribbons
And sawhorses, taking in students
And teachers and the curious pressed
Near the great vandalism of chance.
I told myself to turn away before
The windowsill leaned out and down,
That wall tumbling like a headstone,
The earth swallowing in its ancient way,
Forecasting like the Mother of Mankind,
Who spoke, in Jeddah, for thirty years
From the tomb of Eve. She took questions

Through a slim shaft to the ancient dead,
So far underground, so many coins fed
By foreign pilgrims, she listened
For tone and accent to prepare
The exact change of an answer to send
Up the pneumatic tube for hope.
And there were those who trembled with lust,
Those who offered themselves to her, what
They were willing to do or have done,
Buying queries of blood and semen.
There were those who tunneled until
She used the backdoor to escape
From the warren of secret wants.
And how long should I walk, this evening,
Where traffic is banned? What questions, years
After that school collapsed, should I shout
Through this highway split, finally, from
That mine fire's arrival? What prophecies
Might I hear, following the fire's
Old fissures through the cemetery,
Laying my hands to the smoldering earth
Near the church where the sinkholes plummet
To coal seams burned back to simmering?
Who answers for the future?
In the neighboring field rise rusted rows
Of vents, and no smoke escapes from any,
Moved on, the world beneath them ash.

The
Museum
of
Memory

The Museum of Memory

"Forgetting is the inevitable outcome of all experience."
—GEOFFREY SONNABEND, NEUROPHYSIOLOGIST

"These People," He Says, "I Don't Know."

Passing photos to my father, I wait
For the German names of lost relatives:
Gottlob, Heinrich, three cousins called Otto.
"These people," he says, "I don't know. Do you?"
His grandparents, I think, uncles and aunts
Leaving, perhaps, their poverty behind
At the century's beginning. So here,
The Heinz company picnic, all the men
With beer, standing in suits as if they'd just
Arrived from church. A Sunday, then, summer,
1906, one of the white-shirt boys
My grandfather. "No," my father tells me,
"It's so long ago I don't remember,"
Turning, as well, from the three photographs
Of men in uniform, 1918,
The picnic boys grown up to fight cousins
Who were left behind, my father about
To be born, entering the swelling past.

The Twenty-five Year Trance

*Encephalitis lethargica is an acute inflammatory disease of
the brain characterized by lethargy, weakness, and coma.*

A boy lies down. He hears
His sister say she won't
Shut up and promises
Recovery's revenge.

He moans, tired and hot.
His mother touches his
Forehead, and he tells her
"I could sleep forever."

He sleeps one night and wakes
To an absence of years,
His family transformed
Into doctors for lost time.

All week he's been x'ing
Out lost days: nine thousand.
Nothing will pry open
The coma in his count.

Not his hands, the surprise
Of their age. Not mornings
So stiff he slow paces.
His father is a face

On the wall; his mother
Leans away and says "mumps"

When he asks for a cause,
One more thing he cannot

Believe: her odd German,
His house razed for a church,
How he slept through a war
That repeated the war.

Deja Vu

Just inside the coal door to the cellar
My father coughed while shoveling himself
To black. The air outside waited for him
To finish. I stepped back from spit and NO
To each question about the war—uncles,
Cousins dead in Europe a second time
Because they did not sail. In the yard, once,
After the AirMail asked for money,
My father stood where the cement steps plunged
Thirty-steep to the street and put on
The same look of falling his mother wore
To church. He opened his shirt, and I leaned
To hear what he would say in flight until
He turned strange as the Berlin postmark, red
As if the sun had seared him, bringing up
Blisters like overwork, like a firestorm.

Amusia

After his stroke, my uncle
couldn't recognize a song.
Six hundred wedding receptions

he'd sung at, crooning "Blue Moon"
and "Earth Angel" as often as
the address of the house he found,
once, blindfolded, sensing the length
of seven blocks through the drift
of his car in neutral, turning
between two curbs, parking one foot,
four inches, hand-measured, from
his Frank Sinatra mailbox.
He didn't know "Sincerely"
or "The Way You Look Tonight."
He blinked and wept like the fathers
of brides, astonished at the end
of something, failing the test
of "Happy Birthday" the way
another set of victims
loses the use of numbers,
not knowing what lies between
three and five or the total
for two plus two, each of them
puzzled by the plain and simple
like my mother repeating
"Count your blessings" while she swallowed
six kinds of medicines, able
to sum the good things, writing them
on my unused high-school tablets,
a map of Pennsylvania
on each of thirty-six covers
because I never wrote in them,
certain I'd forget nothing

I heard in a thousand lectures,
since what mattered surely stayed,
all of it said so often
I couldn't lose it if I tried.

Forewarning

Each visit, my father's chair slides
Farther right, the leaves taking more
Of the picture from where I sit,
Refusing to move. By this year,
The single stem in the living room,
Top heavy and leaning like
A weeping birch, sends six leaves
Across the soap opera woman
Who follows her faithless husband
Doubly hidden in the one plant
Surviving my mother's death.
Ten years now, the last three with leaves
On the screen where faces have turned
Purple with disrepair. This time
I see indentations in the carpet,
Circles two inches from the legs.
My father watches the flight of a ball
Into the foliage. A crack runs
Through the corner of the window
Behind him. I imagine a draft,
Tell myself to test with my hand
When he goes to bed. If I want to know
Where the ball lands, I have to listen.

The Durable Word for Wonder

In 1979, in South Africa, a marigold seed sprouted in a boy's eye
—News Item

Our hearts, when we dream, stop beating
As long as nine seconds, testing
The old tale of truly dying
In nightmares, souls straying so far
From bodies they think them strangers.

What do we dream to halt the heart?
Which plot of sex, chase, or falling
Clots the blood and yet vanishes
Like our memories of sunsets,
Scenery, cityscapes, and sky?

What do we know of the discord
Of ocean floors, the harmony
Of atoms, evocative names
For DREAMING we find in the files
Filled with tales of the icon's tears?

Stories of stigmata? When we
Tire of mystery and miracle,
Of signs we must see to explain,
Here is the boy with the flower
In his eye, the small sprout of stem

Shot up as it must, regardless
Of its footing in the warm, damp,

Surrogate soil of the eye.
Here, finally, when the surgeon
Succeeds, when the child is assured

Of sight, his father holds the shoot
Close to his face, says "Marigold"
As if the common name would stop,
Momentarily, our hearts, with
A durable word for wonder.

Foreboding

Citing the four thousand years it's lived,
My father points to a picture
Of a Bristlecone Pine. According
To him, that tree took root after
Noah's Flood to measure the distance
From doom to doom. Listen, he says,
Except for a thin strip of bark where
Sap still rises, this tree is dead.
See? See now? And when I shake my head,
He says, "I don't see who I think
I am," suddenly explaining why,
Past eighty, he turns down mirrors.
His voice, this October, has volume
Only for hymns, but he has me
Drive him, with ham and sweet potatoes,
Green peas and applesauce, to where
He limps those trays to eleven doors,
Leading me, at last, up nine stairs
To a one-chair, television room,
The seated man raising his hand

As if he's asking to be excused.

Younger than me, my father says,

Tugging his hat brim close to his eyes

Until he's settled into shade.

Korsakov's Syndrome

*Amnesia characterized by the inability to record fresh memory
traces, which results in being unable to recall the recent past.*

To reconstruct his meals, the man who forgets the present
leaves his dishes unwashed. Gravy, he thinks in the morn-
ing, mashed potatoes, lima beans, pork. He's wired like an
undercover agent. Tapes everything. In his living room, each
evening, he plays back the recording of his day, trying to
hear himself into his mind. Some nights he hears strangers'
voices claiming friendship. "A key word can be magic,"
someone says. "Thunder. Focus on thunder and listen to your
friends say 'thunder,'" but they lie to the tape, speak like
criminals preparing alibis. He forgives them. He steps out-
side and says "thunder," wondering why it slips out, how
silly the word sounds in 1962 as he shouts it from his drive-
way. "You'll get thunder," his mother warns, "when the Russians
shoot us all down from Cuba." He's going out for basketball;
he's dribbling on the asphalt and listening to the Exciters
sing "Tell Him" while he practices jump shots. His mother, on
the porch, turns down the volume. When he glances up,
thinking, for no reason, of thunder, he is anxious, figuring
that Kennedy's bluff might be called.

Premonition

The last time I saw my father, I dreamed

A restaurant of faceless customers,

Every one of the senses gone but touch.
In the midst of my shouted *no*s, my wife
Woke me and listened, in my old bedroom,
While I named the dead by their body shape
Before they fled to the sensible light.

My wife, when I first knew her, followed me
Into a bar I loved for chili dogs.
Three, I ordered, a large basket of fries,
A pitcher of beer, and Liz humored me,
Smiled and chattered and went so suddenly
Silent I thought she'd choked on an ice cube
From her drink. "What?" I said, rising, but she
Settled me to sitting with a head shake.
I finished two hot dogs with silence, turned,
At last, like a rube, and saw a woman
With no face at the table behind me.
I mean to say everything was concave,
Like someone had driven tires across it.
I mean to say I've never, to this day,
Snapped away faster from staring, but that
Woman, I say now, had more of a face
Than anyone in that dream, though that night
I kept looking at Liz until she said,
"Stop it," and I didn't, not even when
She said, "Suit yourself," and left me behind.

The Unbelievers

Maybe we shouldn't laugh, the rest of us,
When someone like the woman next door says,

"All of us, of course, have been here before."
She means she's already known her daughter,
The problem child, that a mother's mistakes
Are eased through a multitude of chances.
And here we are, the unbelievers, stuck with
The failures of forgetting where we've been
In the previous life of the night before.
This week, on crutches, I weave and wobble
Toward the embarrassment of long-held doors,
My knees becoming my father's as if
I've propped them up before, recognizing
These tiny steps, the terrible importance
Of smiling. I limped, this afternoon, toward
A colleague returned from three months of treatments.
Her eyes told me I believed her dying;
She held her small daughter and didn't say
Anything about seeing her learn to walk
A thousand years ago. These things desert us
When we need them. It's health that drives us crazy.
She used the unimaginable voice
That surprises us; I said the stupid things
About the weather of the following day.

Think of repeating yourself. Go ahead,
You remember. Look back as long as you like.

The
Weaknesses
of
the
Mouth

The Weaknesses of the Mouth

There were punishments for the weaknesses
Of the mouth. Two uncles had killed themselves
With salt and fatty meat; an aunt had slaughtered
Herself with sugar. "Each of them knew,"
My mother declared. I was growing
Into the bone-stunting of tobacco
And candy's pimples. "God's way," according
To my mother, who warned me about
The pack of pink gum I found and chewed,
That there were dope dealers who seeded
Desire with good fortune, waiting for
The next day of need, that gum, alone,
Enough to empty my mouth of teeth.
I stopped talking, then, about the warm dance
Of tongue and lips, the moistures driven
By the heart. The first beer I swallowed
Poured warm from three bottles I found
In the half-razed house where old rubbers
Told me there were willing girls nearby.
I had such weakness I finished a fourth
Long-opened bottle, stepped, minutes later,
Through the lost heat register's empty hole
And stuck at my shoulders instead
Of tumbling to the cellar's glass and nails.
It was the last polio summer,

Seven years until my first cold beer,
Reversing the Pharaoh dream, famine first,
Refusal urging my mouth to open.

The History of Silk

In seventh grade, when we were alone for
An afternoon, no chance of being caught,
Silk was what we sought in our sisters' rooms.
It was enough to hold silk and name girls
Who were slipping off the slick things we touched:
Pajamas, panties, lace-trimmed slips with straps
Designed to be nudged by passionate hands.
Three or four together in those bedrooms,
We turned alike, drawing silk things over
Our skin like fingertips, lifting our shirts,
Opening our pants in dark unisons
Of desire that made us refold those things
Exactly, replacing them in order
Until the afternoon one of us slid
That silk over his head to bring himself
Closer to pleasure, and he did, though none
Of us would touch or talk to him, the words
For his transformed body disappearing
Like faith long before any of us knew
The quiet history of silk, the way
Taming turned the silkworms from tan to white.
The way, defenseless, but unharmed, they stopped
Trying to escape. The way, become moths,
They didn't fly, how they mated and died,
Without once opening their damp, pale wings.

Liverwurst, Headcheese, a List of Loaves

Our refrigerator
Opened to liverwurst,
Headcheese, a list of loaves:
Olive and Old-Fashioned,
The alliteration
Of Luncheon, Luxury,
Peppered, and Pimento.
We eat, my father said,
One hundred million cans
A year, justifying
Our Spam. Three per second,
He figured, and we sat
For sandwiches he cooked
When I refused them cold.
"You just don't know what's good,"
He said, and I agreed,
Completely refusing
Potted Meat Food Product,
Looking it up, lately,
To find "tripe, suet, and
Beef hearts," memorizing
The mystery of
"Partially defatted
Fatty tissue," to tell
My father, who's laid out

Cold cuts to celebrate
His restored heart, shaking
His head at stomachs, snouts,
And the meat byproducts
I recall while we spread
Mustard or mayonnaise,
Add pickles and onions
To the short stack of squares
And circles on thick rye
With seeds. And I listen
To my father repeat
"This is eating" before
Our first bites, smiling while
We swallow extenders
And gelatins, relish
The joy of fat and spice.

Coughing through the Brambles

Some days the asthma wakes me early,
Makes me walk through the underwater dark
And trust my footing to prescriptions
While I find the shallow end of wheezing.
So quiet, this illness, so unlike
The bark of the common cold, the great whoops
Of the cough more serious which killed
One classmate the winter the whooping crane
Stood extinct, almost, on the front page
Of our *Weekly Readers*. We watched slides
Of condors and grizzlies and pale fish
We were supposed to care for, and even now
I watch for Harvey Walker, the sun
An hour away, because his spirit
Might choose to retrace itself, search for
An arrangement of houses and yards
And debris which calls up our childhood,
The dwarf shape of fear whose messages
Stay simple as those folded inside mittens.
For asthma, once, you swallowed spider webs;
For whooping cough, some parents would push
Their children through blackberry brambles,
Those stems which arced to thrust themselves
Back into the ground like living hoops,
Listening to the terrible thrusts
Of air through the constricted hoops of throats.

It was like the laying on of hands
For tumors and tuberculosis;
It was the faith and prayer of my parents
Who passed me through the brambles of eternal
Damnation, expecting answers the way
Some men listen for responses to
Radio waves they transmit to outer space.
The year Harvey Walker died, I read
A story about the first broadcasts
Reflecting off the edge of the universe
And returning for rebroadcasting.
"O, Holy Night," the radios played,
By Professor Fessenden, 1906,
And then Bible verses from St. Luke,
Stutters of stations working toward
The cacophony of perpetual
Retransmission of a billion broadcasts.
And I might pass all of the past's coughing
Through the brambles which run the border
Of the lot I live on, three times each,
One thrust exactly like the others
In distance and direction until
The heavenly white magic takes hold.
And I might lay my healer's hands
On the vulnerable spots of those
I love, trusting the medicinal
Power of faith, but I've weaned myself
From the vanity of prayer, believing
Enough voices are rocketing toward
The imagined edge of the universe,
So many supplications seeking

The thin, improbable antenna,
The unlikely decoding, and then,
So far to return, so many requests,
The everlasting shower of granted
Wishes soaking the astonished
Descendants of the faithful and
The faithless, flooding both with bitterness
And joy, and drowning the need to believe.

Miss Hartung Teaches the Importance of Fruit

The banana is a herb, she said, but
The Koran claims it's the forbidden fruit.
The orange is a berry. Grapefruit is new.
On Fridays, when we opened our lunches,
She lectured on our apples, plums, and grapes.

A president, she said, after hogging
Cherries, died; a French king, over-anxious,
Bit the prickly skin of a pineapple
And shredded his greedy lips. Remember,
She said, tomatoes and olives are fruit:

Eat your salads and think of them as sweet.
She brought papayas, mangoes, kiwi, figs.
She taught the origin of the lemon
And the domestication of the lime.
She said there are 5,000 kinds of pears,

Doctors who prescribe them like booster shots.
Pick them early, she warned us, or they go
Gritty; let them ripen in your kitchens
Or the cells inside them will turn to stone.
Listen, children, she said in June, the peach

Preserves the body. The Spanish brought them,
And even the Indians learned to love that fruit.
And why not, don't all of us know the way
To everlasting life? Don't we all have
An instinct for the perfect gift from God?

During Sixth Grade

We learned the Redcoats lost to Patriots
Who wore drab hand-me-downs and mended rags.
We memorized the spellings of handsome
And beautiful, vanity and conceit.
Miss Blatt said listen to this lesson: birds
With the brightest feathers are attacked first
By their predators. We wrote it down so
We wouldn't forget the consequences
Of fame. We passed around her photographs
Of Harlow and Valentino, starting
An album which stopped at the red jacket
Of James Dean, who the year before had been
Pecked by the great beak of our jealous God.
I memorized the size and shape of each
Sixth-grade bra cup and thought Sarah Nestel
Would surely die before the rest of us.
My father, the troop leader, testified
To the character of a Boy Scout who
Confessed, at last, to a series of rapes
As if any girl's body had beauty
Enough to attack. The homely brother
Of a classmate crashed his old car and died.
The perfect proportion of bright plumage
To death broke like schoolbook bindings; nothing
Excluded me from the spell of disbelief.

Johnny Weissmuller Learns the Tarzan Yell

For public appearances, for the crowds
Who expected perfection, he managed,
Take after take, to mimic the sound
The studio had built for an ape-child.
Practice was like swimming all those laps
In the pool, building his breath again
To fill the audio needs of Tarzan:
Camel's bleat, hyena howl played backwards—
He couldn't admit to plucked violin,
A soprano's high C added, one
After the other, to his own best roar,
His champion's howl so much a common cry
The audience wouldn't think "explorer caught
In quicksand," "hunter surrounded by spears,"
Not Tarzan loud in the natural world
Where the hybrid voice develops into
The great arpeggio of beast and man.

Dialogues

We wrote for Miss Price. We made voices
That weren't ours for three full pages:
The old, the immigrants, Negroes, Jews.

We used the lost L of Japanese.
We jabbered in broken Spanish.
One of us wrote a comical pope.

We read our conversations aloud,
And all of us listened to the words
Of Communists, Italians, and bums.

Everyone in English kept smiling:
The Polish, the Catholics, the sons
And the daughters of the unemployed.

In Berlin, where my cousins were
Divided, the new wall was guarded
By men who said nothing in our homework.

I didn't write German. I knew how
It sounded, all coughs and commands,
The clearing in my grandfathers' throats.

When I read the words of Tyrone
And Sapphire, Miss Price gave me an A
For drawl and dialect and humor.

Those city folk had so much to say,
I improvised after class. I could talk
And talk like someone I'd never met.

School was as easy as not listening.
I was a good student. I repeated
What I didn't know until I'd learned it.

The History of SAC

1952

In the hospital, in the enormous ward,
Forty-eight iron lungs were breathing for
The tri-state's victims. Nurses paused to murmur
Near each disembodied head, the room
A theater of whispers, the film obscure.
My aunt, their supervisor, held my hand.
I breathed in and out through my sterile mask
And thought of steam irons at the dry cleaners,
My father's two suits tagged and returned
Like pigeons. The smell of trichloroethylene,
How it dizzied, how it followed us
For a half-block of storefronts. On runways,
At that moment, thousands of bombers
Were idling in case Truman or Stalin
Decided to end the world. In the sky,
To our north, a shift of squadrons hung
Like the mobile over the face of the boy
In the row to my right, second lung.

1972

We drove to a runway's end, the great
Passenger planes lifting six minutes apart,
Banking and turning toward selected cities
Like missiles. We parked and faced the squat cliff

Like the disembarked; the sky became
A belly so heavy it had to fall.
That evening, you clutched yourself by the stove,
The front, right burner coiled red under
A saucepan poised for boiling. Wait a while,
You said, let's see, and turned the water to LOW.
After the coils went dark, you said
"Yes, again" and disappeared to dress.
The plates and silverware lay bare three days.
A nurse walked the aisles among the isolettes,
So many babies breathing so easily,
I listened for the heavy approach
Of apprehension, the water in the pan
Transformed to air, the kitchen turned metallic,
The stove sitting ready as a SAC bomber,
Idling on LOW until you handed me
Our son and dialed it slowly down to OFF.

1992

In the AIDS unit, we walk with my sister,
Who has a grant, hundreds of thousands
Of dollars, to study the attitudes
Of care for these lethal patients, the poor,
Twenty to a side. I keep to the center,
Curse myself as I do when I refuse
The sturdy rails at overlooks, dilettante
Of the blood. I think of yours in that instant
Which fixes us to eternity,
That son old enough to contract disease
From his ward approach to sex, and when we

Reboard at America's newest airport,
Enough runways to handle the SACs
Of a hundred nations, my childless sister
Says, "We're going global," sweeping her hand
As if she means to peel off the horizon.

Stealing the Saints

The last year my father expected me
In church, I slept with a Catholic girl
Who was afraid all of her thoughts were taped
For extended play in the court of God.
She was earning, she said, a room in Hell,
By dreaming constantly of suicide.
There were prayers to save the natural dead,
She said, listing leukemia and stroke,
But nothing to save the volunteer dead,
Though one late evening she pressed against me
In my Plymouth and marked the headlights of
Approaching trucks before she whispered "Now."

I was crazy myself with fantasies
Of mortality, months into 1-A
For Vietnam's draft, but when she shuddered,
Her tongue in my ear, I started to speed,
Clocking forty-five second miles while lights
Flared and passed and vanished like the future.
I thought I was changing into someone
Who could sacrifice himself for pleasure,
But some other boy rolled her and himself
In her father's Mercury, both of them
Thrown clear, unhurt, an hour before she called
To fret about the luck of pitch and roll.

I thought she'd saved my life by crashing with
Someone who expected eternity.
Dumped in her driveway, that torn car seduced
The near-death crowd, but her father, because
She hadn't asked his permission, meant it
As an icon for the consequences
Of theft. "Steal it, Gary," she begged, as if
I would snatch that wreck from Hell's examples,
But I drove past like a dreadful neighbor
And kept everything I knew to myself,
Including what I'd been reading about
The history of thieving in her church,
How one parish stole the remains of saints

From another, hauling the holy bones
Home for luck. Blessed were the monasteries
Where skeletons of the saved were displayed,
Attracting tourists for another kind
Of escape-from-death. Blessed, then, was her house,
But even if I scoffed that night, saying
Goodbye to one avoidable danger,
I realized those priests wanted to insure
Certainty by building holy theme parks
For pilgrims, keeping watch over the bones
And constructing history, counting on
Their promises to be centuries long.

Zombies

It was the year of zombie movies, dead bodies
Without brains that wanted the blood of the living.

It was the year, at my school, of five student deaths,
The principal acknowledging three of them through
Counseling, assemblies, and a week of silent
Moments for the regents scholar, the soccer star,
And the girl who checked my groceries after school.

One of the two whose deaths were not announced was
killed
On a motorcycle, thrown into a phone pole
After a skid and rollover. The other, drunk,
Stumbled in front of a truck, their names short-listed
With the absentees under *Deceased: Please Delete.*
They didn't read, those boys whose deaths were not
announced.
They didn't listen, those boys, "And truthfully now,"
The principal said, "are you going to miss them?"

It was the year of the dead who wanted to eat
The brains of the living, the natural logic
Of the empty head. How easily hatreds talked
And talked. There were teachers who read that absence list
Like a stock report, cheering extended illness.

The friends of those boys said nothing about silence
In homeroom, a day off, or an oak tree planted
In memory. They kept hate to themselves until
They could drink it into speech among themselves—slurs
Spoken in cars, expletives underage in bars,
The curses that followed fists to the stunned faces
Of each other, not to the principal's they loathed,
The teachers' they'd delete, if there was any choice
In who lived and died in the lottery of luck.

That boy whose brains were spilled against a roadside post,
That boy whose brains were splattered under a truck tire—
All along they'd been brainless in the back of class,
But I thought of them rising when Three Mile Island
Leaked into our lives; I thought of the school downwind,
The dead getting second chance by radiation
The way they do in B-movies, the principal
Keeping the school in session the full day because
He believed (Who wouldn't? he said) the spokesperson.
When, the next week, I dialed in sick from Virginia,
I knew he'd call my house, checking, on the third day.
Which didn't matter, since those boys, looking for brains,
Would crack his skull and slurp him down. Wasn't he smart?
Hadn't he known all along how they would turn out?

The Top Bunk of a Ford

I should have ended on the cracked asphalt
Of stupidity when the heavy Ford
Backed over my drunk and sleeping body.
Hours earlier, I'd had a chance to choose
The common sense of shutting down my mouth,
But I'd slurped two dozen beers and slurred out
My complaints about the shit-war and where
America wanted me to spend it.
I had two semesters left in one kind
Of R&R, and I owed principal
And interest on immaturity's loan,
But when I sprawled to sleep on that driveway,
I was planning to repay no one but myself.
I should say I woke believing I was
Rising for an early class, but I knew
I was under the top bunk of a Ford,
That whoever was dragging me from sleep
Wasn't sending me to work. "Jesus Christ,"
I heard, "Goddamn it to hell" and the rest
Of profanity's trite variations,
And I was calculating, sitting up
Beside that car, how few inches that Ford
Needed to turn to crush some part of me.
I said nothing to the driver who'd braked,
The passenger who'd rolled down his window

To swallow the air as soon as that Ford
Hit reverse, but I listened to enough
Eyewitness testimony to prove
I'd hit the quinella of good fortune,
Memorized the tread of the right front tire
Which would surely, while turning, have made me
Exhibit A for the consequences
Of bad judgment. And then those two sat down
Beside me, the three of us leaning back
Against the Ford and saying nothing while
We faced the brightening sky as if we had
Chosen an alternate way to be awestruck.

In Films, the Army Ants Are Always Intelligent

Water and fire again, we think, watching
Natives dig a trench, lug the gasoline
To its banks. It's the white man's solution,
Some landowner protecting investments,
All those years of cheap labor just lately
Paying off. Ants, after all, are ants, but
Understandably, he's a bit nervous
When his workers chant, fumble with magic
In a pouch. Savages, he's learned, always
Sense when the absentee gods should be called.

And we might wonder, while the cameras pan
The rain forest for troops, if these things rest,
If there's a day along the Amazon
When you could sleep off hard work or a drunk
In safety. And why there's still a jungle;
And why these ants, a million years of them,
Haven't eaten every square inch of green.
There's never a natural predator;
There's only the good sense of travel north
So climate can negotiate with them.

All we're taught, at last, are the miles of them,
That their sign language ripples front to back,
Reaching the billionth soldier correctly.
Remember that schoolroom game, the one where

Miss Harshman whispered a message into
Janey's ear, who turned and whispered those words
To Billy, who whispered to Sally, and
Thirty seats later you recited them
To laughter that blossomed from the first row?

Think of yourself as sluggard in the rear.
For days you've had nothing to eat, the ground
You're covering stripped clean ten thousand ranks
Before you. Well, somebody has to starve,
You might conclude, improvisational
In the tropics. But then you feel the word,
Sense *plantation, panic, picnic for all.*
So there's sacrifice ahead; there's something
To those parables, you see, when your turn
Finally comes: The early waves were burnt;
The first leaf rafts were sunk; and you're certain,
Dancing before battle, that the water
And fire are gone, that the natives have fled
Or been shot in the back by the owner.
So he's on his own now, self-destructive,
Or maybe he has dynamite, something
Apocalyptic. On the other side
Of the moat there is feasting. All you have
To do is cross, stepping from one body
To another, to cultivated land.

Finding Harvey Kelly in the Former Sanitarium

I toured the college from which I was fired.
I left the library for the short walk
To my office where six names, according
To my friend, have slid out of the nameplate
On the door. Twenty-two years, and he sat
In his third chair behind his second desk,
But he named no faces in the halls, stopped
At the door of the man who dismissed me,
That president, he said, gone in scandal,
The dean who told me subsequently fired.
We tried the steepness of the oldest stairs;
We passed the south side's floor-to-ceiling glass,
So much sanitarium sunlight, once,
To promote the greenhouse effect of hope.
We offered stories from our years-old files
While we walked, annotating locations
We wished to save. Deep in some ancient tombs,
He told me, white walls show no trace of soot,
Yet you see the unmarred work of artists.
The light of the sun was carried to them
By mirrors, reflection of reflection,
The angles just so, the slaves who held them
Moving together to keep the sunlight
In those studios, choreographing

The smokeless air of artistry. And then,
Near the windowless end of one hallway,
The chopped name of someone I remembered:
VEY KEL, the beginning and the ending
Gone to the grease of a thousand touchings,
And I started a story, how, in France,
Some students cleaning graffiti from caves
Erased the art of the Neanderthals,
And nothing can be done to restore it.

Giants

After Creation, in the last chapter
Before the flood, is the short-short story
Of those Nephilim, the angels who fell

From grace for the bodies of women who
Suffered, in turn, giving birth to the giants
In the earth, everything in vain because

Shortly thereafter, they drowned for their sins
In the deluge, none of them saved like apes.
Listen, the philosopher Henrion

Calculated the heights of Genesis:
Adam first, one hundred twenty-three feet.
Then Eve, one hundred eighteen, beginning

Our descent from height, each generation
Shorter until, says Henrion, God stopped
Before we turned "mere atoms on the earth."

Think of Goliath, nine feet, nine inches,
His army so short he was predestined
By the military's demand for height.

Think of Nimrod, who brought diversity
To language and was banished, for discord,
To the lowest circle of Dante's Hell.

Sure, he was a guard, what suits the giants,
But always someone misuses their bones,
Believing the deceptive evidence

Of fossils. Boccaccio, for instance,
Extrapolating the Cyclops from skulls
Until the objective said "elephants."

So science shortens us with proof's yardstick,
Calling out the verifiable names:
Robert Wadlow, an inch below nine feet;

Jane Bunford, seven feet, seven inches,
The tallest we've stood against the door frame
Of scrutiny, those photographed giants

Dying so young we chalk-mark our children,
Placing our fingers on the increments
Like parents who must measure to believe.

The Details of the Soil

Not yet, I haven't taken a bite,
But the woman who offers me clay
Says "Go on," and waits as if I am
Sniffing at the end of a leash.

The dirt eaters she knows are hundreds
Of miles from her driveway, and they've sent,
For her birthday, the local clay
She craves. "Go on," she advises,

"It's good for what ails you," quoting
My mother who spooned baking soda
To water to bring up the acids
Of bad habits. Between my fingers

The clay turns the primary shade
Of silence. "Our faith," my mother said,
"Begins in mud." She meant me to kneel.
She meant me to pay attention

To the details of the soil,
Acidity, depth, and texture,
How likely it was to retain
Our region's brief, sporadic rain.

During the last summer I helped
Her plant, I crouched in the front row
Of a crowd come to watch women
Wrestle in measured, weekly mud.

They wore bikinis we expected
To tear; a man stood by with a hose
Through half nelsons and leg scissors,
Bear hugs, body slams, the spraying

Of our pants and shirts with splotches
We wiped with our hands, wetting the tips
Of our fingers in our whiskeyed mouths.
And I have learned, since then, there are frogs

Who mistake some mounds of mud for mates.
And because they never enter,
They croak and squeeze, coaxing the eggs
To easy sites for their ready sperm.

How long can anyone be fooled?
Think of the patience of fondling,
The instinctive working of mud
To shapes so perfect it does not

Matter if a season of eggs
Oozes from such beauty, the future
Suddenly as irrelevant as signs
Of pleasure from the pliable dirt.

The Limber Buildings

All the skyscrapers that sway more than most
have a P-Delta moment, the possible point of
collapse when weakness, weather, or weapons
attack.

So often, we need to test resilience,
How much the heart can take, as if it were
A tall building that has to handle wind,
Its speed and angle, things that threaten height.

Sunday, leaving New York, we stopped speaking.
That refusal, from pride, from anger, stretched
Until Tuesday morning when planes-as-bombs
Resurrected our speech to seek the sound

Of our children's voices from three cities.
That day and the next, talking and talking,
We were new to each other again, filled
With words for the daughter we could not reach,

The Manhattan child I'd wanted to slap
For declaring me selfish, ranking it
The best of my sins, as if she could count
The hours I justified my silences.

And then, from safety, she talked as calmly
As a high-rise engineer explaining

"Close to instability" in language
Designed to mute our terror, revealing

The surprise of what saves us, those we love
Untangling themselves from ruins that shift
And shudder and steady, then open to
An extraordinary pocket of light.

Descending with Bagpipes

Holding their bagpipes like babies,
Twenty kilted men fly with us
From Cincinnati to New York.
For ten minutes, I think about
Instruments slipping through checkpoints,
The odds of bagpipe terrorists,
And then I make myself finish
A novella about the need
For revenge, how education
Doesn't keep a teacher like me
From killing somebody for blood.
Two pages from the end, I hear
One squall, suddenly a second,
Despair being tuned and tested
Through the recirculated air.
In the aisle, two of the men stand
Like stewards, and from the cockpit,
Like an emcee, the pilot says
These men will serenade the plane's
Descent. I finish two pages
To scales; I finish the story
To the first notes of what I thought
Would be "Amazing Grace," the hymn
Bagpipers always play in films.
The woman next to me whispers,

"Will we see it?" And when I say,
"See what?" she says, "You know, the mess
They made out of the Trade Center."
"Yes," I say, "you can see it," and
They play one of those Scottish airs,
Something sad I can only name
By genre, that woman leaning
Across me to stare, her seat belt
Undone as we start to descend,
Those two bagpipers still standing
In the aisle, bleating that ancient,
Familiar song as if we need
To be comforted as we sink
Beneath the brilliant, cloudless air.